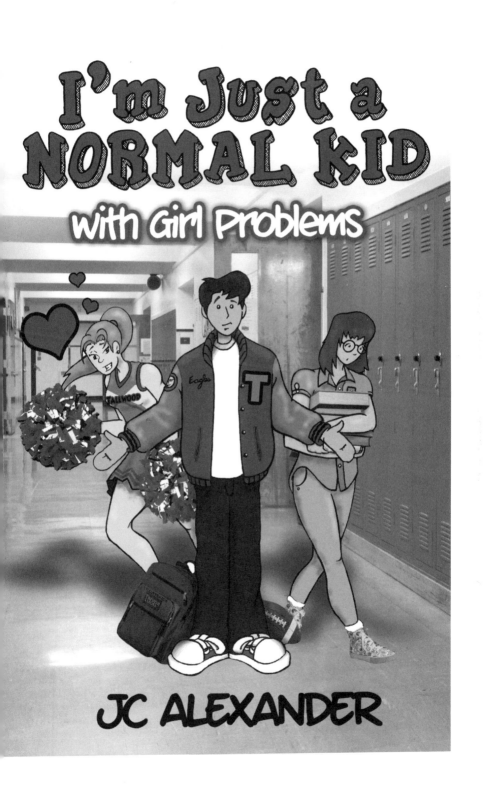

I'm Just a Normal Kid with Girl Problems

This is a work of fiction. All of the characters, organizations, and events portrayed in this novel are either products of the author's imagination or are used fictitiously.

Publisher's address:

K.S. Publications
P.O. Box 68878
Virginia Beach, VA 23471

Website: www.ImJustaNormalKid.com
Email: KS.publications@yahoo.com

ISBN-13: 978-0985349561
ISBN-10: 0985349565

First Edition: August 2013

10 9 8 7 6 5 4 3 2 1

Editors: Letitia Carrington & Kelly Walker-White
Interior Layout: Davida Baldwin (OddBalldsgn.com)
Illustrator & Cover Design: Trevor Lucas

Printed in the United States of America

To my children, Kamryn & John,

this is for you.

Dear Fans,

Thank you for giving me a chance to show you that popular and nerdy kids can coexist. It's okay for a popular guy to like a nerdy girl. And it's also okay for a popular girl to have a crush on a less popular guy. Or any other guy for that matter because everyone has a heart. So, put your egos to the side and enjoy the ride.

At the end of this story, log onto www.ImJustANormalKid.com & let me know what you thought about the story.

Yours truly,

JC Alexander

ARE YOU TEAM LAUREN

"I am the envy of all girls and I love it."

"It takes beauty and popularity to walk in my shoes. A lot of the not-so-popular girls wished they could be like me. But it would never happen"

ARE YOU TEAM DILLON

"I'm one of the most popular guys in school and beside Tony Hawk & Rob Dyrdek, I'm the best skate boarder in the world."

"I can have any girl I want but I'm tired of the shallow girls. I want a girl friend who's not so popular. But I'm afraid my friends may not want to hang out with me anymore."

ARE YOU TEAM
MEGAN

"Why can't I be pretty like the popular girls?"

"Why is that I can't go out with the popular guys? I would give away everything I have to be pretty and hot. I just want to belong. Am I asking for the impossible?"

ARE YOU TEAM ZACH

"I'm Dillon's best friend and his right hand man."

"We only date popular girls and we're good at it. Girls literally stand in line to go out with us. We have girls eating out of our hands"

Chapter One - Dillon

Life couldn't get any better. My best friend Zach and I were two of the most popular kids in school. We were both skateboard champions and we could go out with any girl in school. The choices were plentiful. Girls would literally stand in line for the chance to be in the company of Zach or myself. They'd even pay us to date them if we wanted them to. So when Zach called me from his iPhone and told me we had a new babe moving into our neighborhood, I was eager to check out my new prospect. "Look out of your bedroom window. She's getting out of the car with her parents right now," he instructed me.

Zach was a part of our neighborhood watch. Well, he wasn't officially a part of the adult's association, so he kind of made up his own club since he saw almost everything that went on and around our neighborhood. "Oh my God! I see

her legs." Zach whispered as if he'd spoken any louder she'd hear him.

"Do you see how big her dad is?" I asked Zach.

"Of course I do, he's blocking my view!" Zach responded sarcastically.

"Why don't cha' yell and tell him to move?" I laughed.

"And watch how our whole operation goes up in smoke, I don't think so."

"Hey, look he's moving..." I interjected and then we both fell silent. "Oh my God! I see her!" I continued after I got a full view of her entire body.

"Tell me she's not the most beautiful girl in the world and I will personally vote you out of the club." Zach warned me.

The new girl walked in front of her dad and headed towards their front door. My eyes were glued to the way she glided up the sidewalk. To see her hair blow in the wind was magical. I couldn't believe my eyes. Zach was right. She was a freaking knockout! Her hair was long, blonde and curly. And her skin looked smooth as a newly paved road. I could only wonder how she got so beautiful. "Dillon, I think I'm in love." Zach commented.

"I think I'm in love too." I replied as we both daydreamed about holding her in our arms.

"Well, let's make a wager on who gets her first." Zach suggested.

"Oh no! Keep your money. I can't ever have another episode of your mom beating down my front door. My parents busted my chops for hours after your mom told them you had gambled all your lunch money away to me." I began to re-iterate.

Making bets were common between Zach and I. Occasionally we'd make wagers on who'd do the best skateboard tricks at the skate park and Zach always ended up on the losing side.

By JC Alexander

#What can I say? He was the biggest loser in the world!

"Tell you what, whoever gets her phone number first must do the other's homework for one entire week." Zach suggested.

"Okay. That sounds fair. When do we start?" I wanted to know. Zach was a very competitive guy and he took it hard whenever he'd lose a bet against me. Zach was a sore loser period. The only reason why he and I were friends was because we hung out at the same skate park and we lived on the same block.

"Let's start now," he replied.

"Are you sure you wanna do this? You could definitely save yourself some time and the embarrassment by starting my homework assignments tonight." I said confidently.

"Yeah, sure I'll start on it. But make sure you give it to your mom before she leaves the house to come over and give me a foot massage."

"Not on your life Shrek! My dad would bury you alive if he knew you had the hots for his wife." I commented.

"Correction sport! Your mom has the hots for me."

While Zach was making outlandish comments about my mother, I blocked him out and searched our beautiful new neighbor's face and noticed that she looked a few years older than Zach and myself. This major mix-up could derail my chances of winning the bet. So I immediately re-directed his attention back to our new neighbor. "Zach, do you see what I see?" I asked him.

"What is it?"

"I don't think she's going to be gracing the hallways of our school. She looks at least two years older than us. And you of all people know that if she got us by a couple of years, we'd get

snubbed the first time she noticed us checking her out."

"Don't speak too fast Einstein. Let me do some investigating and I'll call you back."

"Hurry up."

"Patience lover boy. Patience."

"Call me back as soon as you get the word."

"Will do." Zach assured me and then he disconnected our call.

Immediately after my chat with Zach ended, I sat there and stared out the window and watched my future girlfriend as she strolled up to her parent's new home. It was an enjoyment to see the wind blow through her hair. She was definitely my kind of girl and I vowed to make sure she knew it.

"Dillon, it's lunch time." I heard my mother yell from the kitchen.

"I'll be down in a minute mom." I yelled without taking my eyes off the blonde beauty from across the street. I watched her as she helped her parents carry several grocery bags into the house.

Immediately after my blonde babe disappeared into her house I zipped down to the kitchen where my mom was destroying what culinary dreams she had left. The kitchen was literally engulfed in smoke. I fanned my way to the kitchen table where she had my grilled cheese sandwich awaiting my arrival. As soon as I took a seat the smoke detector went off. ERRR...ERRRR....ERRR. It sounded like a police siren. It ranged out throughout the entire kitchen. My mother hopped on top of one of the kitchen chairs with a hand towel in one hand and tried to fan away the smoke. "Mom do you want me to do that?" I yelled.

"No baby, I got it. Just eat your lunch before it gets cold." She yelled back. This was her way of making sure I heard her loud and clear.

I had to admit that my mom was a basket case. I couldn't believe she was worried about

my lunch getting cold. She should've been more concerned about me dying from smoke inhalation. I stood up from the kitchen chair. "Seriously mom, we need to get out of this house before we both die."

"Dillon honey, stop with the exaggeration. We only have a little smoke problem." She explained. My mother was a straggly, thin lady who'd try to save the world if she could. All she needed was a red cape strapped to her back and she'd be the next superhero.

"Do you have any last words?" I asked her. I felt it was my duty to tell the rest of the family her last and final words. I mean that was the least I could do under the circumstances.

"Dillon stop distracting me. I've got to get this smoke under control," she replied as she continued to fan the smoke away from the smoke detector.

"Well, I'm gonna be outside if you change your mind." I told her. I figured if the house was

going to burn down then it was going down without me.

"Take your lunch with you." She yelled over the alarm.

#Is she freaking serious right now? That sandwich is contaminated!

 9

By JC Alexander

Chapter Two - Zach

I skated over to Dillon's house on my Tony Hawk skateboard. I did a couple of heel and kick flips the second I came within five yards of his front yard just in case the new beautiful, blonde neighbor happened to be looking out of her bedroom window. I've been told that you're never given a second chance to make a first impression. Dillon and I had a bet going so the pressure was on. "Why are you looking like you lost your best friend?" I cracked a smile. Dillon was looking kind of weird.

"I just escaped from a burning house. How else would I look?" he commented.

"I take it your mom was trying to cook again."

"Yeah, she was. And if my dad was home he'd ban her from the kitchen altogether."

I hopped off my skateboard and took a seat next to Dillon on his porch. We both stared at the house directly across the street. "Think she has a boyfriend?" Dillon asked me.

"If she does, you're screwed." I replied.

"No, we're both screwed."

"Speak for yourself. I'm a hopeless romantic. Girls can't resist me." I told him as I glanced into the sky.

Dillon burst into laughter. "Yeah, Gabriella couldn't resist you either. Remember she told everyone in school that you two made out after the football game? I think your stock went up like two cents a share after that."

"Don't remind me." I frowned. Thinking about how Gabriella almost ruined my reputation gave me a nauseating feeling in my stomach. It took me almost a whole school year to settle a

few bribes to get back in the good graces of my peers.

"Hey wait, did you find out if she's going to our school or not?"

"My sources haven't gotten back with me. But they will. Don't worry."

Moment's later Dillon's mother opened the front door. She looked disoriented and her clothes were in disarray. Dillon's family may need to call an intervention. The lady looked like she had just had an alien encounter. I sat there and looked at her in amazement. "Hi Zach," she smiled.

"Hi Mrs. Carmichael," I replied. But in my mind I was laughing at how weird she looked.

"How's your mother?"

"I'm not sure. But I know she's not burning down our house."

Dillon punched me in the arm while Mrs. Carmichael chuckled. "You kids are so hilarious." She said and she turned her attention to-

wards Dillon. "Honey, you didn't eat your lunch. And now it's cold."

#She had me sitting inside of a gas chamber with a burnt grilled cheese sandwich. Talk about torture!

"Mom, the conditions of the kitchen weren't exactly user friendly. Believe me, I would've died before I had the chance to eat half of my sandwich."

"Well, you know your dad doesn't like it when you waste food so I'll wrap it up and put it in the refrigerator for later."

Dillon let out a long sigh. "All right, mom."

Okay, well you kids behave." Mrs. Carmichael said and then she closed the front door.

Dillon and I turned our attention back to the house across the street. He and I were in deep thought until I said, "I wonder if her parents allow her to date."

"Why don't you just go on over there and ask?"

"Hey look, she's coming outside." I announced as my heart started beating more rapidly than normal. The last time my heart raced at this speed was when I thought my math teacher Mrs. Barton had caught me cheating on her math test.

"She's looking over here." Dillon sounded alarmed. And then he turned his head. I turned my head too.

#It's not cool for a guy to get caught gawking at a hot girl.

That's **Rule #3** in the **How to Date a Hot Girl** manual. Dillon and I both acted like we were looking at something down the block from his house. But did I mention that we had our peripheral visions working in overdrive?

"Is she still looking at us?" I asked him.

"No, she's getting something out of her parent's car."

"What is she doing now?" My questions continued.

"She's going back in the house now." Dillon told me. So, I turned my attention towards her. I figured this would be the best time to take in more of her physical beauty. She was perfect.

15

And all I needed was for her to be my girlfriend and my life would be complete.

Once she disappeared into her house again, Dillon and I couldn't stop talking about her. She was surely a knockout and she was my neighbor, which gave me easy access. Of course Dillon would dispute that fact, but who cared?

Not too long after my blonde beauty went inside of her parent's house, our attention was diverted to this girl riding her bike. When she looked over at Dillon and I she lost her balance and fell off her bike. I burst into laughter. But lover boy ran to her rescue.

"Are you okay?" I heard Dillon ask her as he helped her get her bike off the ground.

"Why don't you give her a kiss Romeo? I'm sure it'll make her feel a lot better." I yelled. The girl's name he helped was Meagan. She lived at the end of our block. She also attended our school. But we didn't hang out with her because she wasn't on the hot list. She'd need a drastic

makeover to get me to look at her for more than five minutes. She was definitely not my type.

I'd let her carry my books & do my homework. But that was it.

 17

By JC Alexander

Chapter Three - Dillon

My dad finally came home after playing a few games of golf with his investment buddies. My sister Julie came home a few minutes later with her best friend Molly. Julie and Molly were seniors at their high school and they were always up to no good. She played this innocent role around my parents but I knew what went on in her bedroom. Skyping topless in front of her laptop computer for a bunch of morons in her senior class to gain the homecoming queen vote was the dumbest idea she could've ever mustered up. Zach caught his older brother Matt and a few of his pals drooling in front of his computer monitor during one of my sister's strip teases. Zach even came clean and told me how he hid underneath his brother's bed a few time so he could see her from start to finish. "She starts at the exact same

18

time everyday like she's on regular TV. All that's missing are a few commercials." He told me. For a few seconds, he reminded me of a dirty old man. The thought of it almost made me throw up in my mouth.

#That was definitely a "TMI" moment.

"Dillon have you been in my room?" My sister Julie yelled from the other side of my bedroom door.

I was sitting on the floor of my bedroom, playing with my Xbox Kinect when my sibling from hell interrupted me. "No, I haven't." I yelled back.

"So, tell me why my closet door is open?"

By JC Alexander

"Dude, why don't you ask mom?" I yelled once again. All I wanted her to do was catch the hint that I didn't want to be bothered.

#I wanted to open my door &give her the finger, but I didn't want to interrupt my game.

She punched my door. "I know you're lying. Just stay out of my room." She screamed.

I ignored her and continued playing my game. Believe it or not, my sister was a drama queen. In her own little perfect world, everything revolved around her. Unfortunately for her, I had enough common sense to know that she was psychotic and delusional. Remind me to put an "*En-ter at Your Own Risk*" sign on her door.

#Beware my sister is one red nose short of being a clown!

Not too long after my sister Julie left my bedroom door harassing me, my dad decided he wanted to talk. He knocked on my door twice. "Dillon, I need to talk to you son." He said.

I dreaded getting up to open the door, but I knew he wasn't going to go anywhere until he had his say. Whatever that was. My dad had the tendency to go on and on about things that didn't make much sense to a kid my age. But I listened anyway. "Have you met our new neighbors?" he asked me immediately after he walked into my room.

I stood there and looked at him from head to toe. My dad was a pretty short guy. He was also

a suit and tie guy. And to make matters worse, he thought he was cool.

#Can you say weirdo?

"No, I haven't met them. But I saw them unloading a few things from their car not too long ago." I told him.

"Your mother just baked them a pie. I think you 'ought to go over there with her when she goes to welcome them into the neighborhood. Who knows, their daughter may get the hots for you." He smiled.

I immediately became grossed out when I saw all the leftover meatloaf from last night's dinner barricaded between my dad's teeth. In my opinion he needed to be more concerned about flossing than about whether or not I'd accompany my mother when she makes a b-line to our neighbor's house.

He also needed to be concerned about my mom's pie. I figured once they take the first bite of her pie, they'd probably take out restraining orders on all of us. Talk about a major disaster!

"Dad, allowing mom to take them one of her pies isn't a very good idea. You know she can't boil a pot of hot water without the smoke detector going off."

My dad snickered. "I've already taken care of that." He whispered. "I stopped by the local supermarket and picked up one of those frozen apple pies. Now if your mother pops it in the oven and screws that up then we're gonna have to put her on landscaping duties."

I took a seat on the edge of my bed. "What's really going on dad?" I asked. If I hadn't known any better, I would think that he was scheming. For what, I couldn't tell you. But knowing my dad, he had something up his sleeves.

My dad took a step closer to me. "Nothing. I just want you to check out the new bombshell be-

fore someone else snatches her right from under you."

"Come on dad, you know I can get any girl I want." I replied confidently.

"Yes son I know that. But, there is something special about that girl across the street. And I don't think you should be dragging your feet on it."

I watched my dad as he ran down his plan of attack. He always tried to school me on how to ask a girl out. My dad would never admit it, but my mother told me that he wasn't the most popular kid in school. And now that he has a son who's very popular, he was somewhat living vicariously through me.

To get my dad off my back I agreed to go with my mother to our new neighbor's house. He snickered like a little kid and gave me a few more pointers before he exited my room.

"When she looks at you make sure you stand tall like I taught you. You're representing the

Carmichaels. And before you leave make sure you two exchange numbers."

My dad looked more excited about our neighbor's daughter than I was. I knew he meant well. But he needed to chill out. I knew how to talk to girls. And I also knew that I'd lose major cool points if I tagged along with my mother just so she could drop off a cheesy apple pie.

#That would be a dummy move!

I ended up ditching my mother and headed out to the skate park to hang out with a couple of school buddies. Zach was there on his board executing a ton of flips and turns. He was an awesome skateboarder but he was no match for me. He knew I was the master. So immediately after I got inside of the bowl and picked up my speed,

By JC Alexander

I did a Caballerial and a McTwist, and all the attention at the park zoomed in on me. What a cool feeling that was.

Chapter Four - Zach

Dillon and I were the go-to-guys in school that other guys came to with *girl problems*. We were like relationship gurus but on a much smaller scale. I mentioned to Dillon a few times about how we needed to get paid for our relationship advice. We'd have more than just allowance money stuffed away underneath our mattresses if he'd listen to me.

Yesterday he and I made a bet about who'd be the first to get our new neighbor's phone number. And today, marked day two of our mission so the pressure was on.

Dillon was staring into his locker when I cruised down the hallway. He didn't see me coming so I snuck up behind him and grabbed onto his belt near the spine of his back and pulled

his pants in an upward motion, causing his underwear to give him a huge wedgey.

"Hey dude, cut it out." Dillon barked as he turned to face me. To prevent any of the other kids from seeing him pull his pants out of his butt, he backed himself close towards his locker.

"Don't be so uptight lover boy." I chuckled.

"Hey dude, don't you have a classroom to fall asleep in?"

"Nope. I promised my parents that I'd pay more attention and focus in all of my classes this week provided that they pitch in to help me get new wheels for my skateboard this weekend."

"Why don't you promise them that you'll actually do some school work too and then maybe they'll throw in some new wheels for me too." Dillon said and then he turned back towards his locker.

"Oh there's no way they'll believe me if I said that. The last time I did my class work was a year ago when I first entered into the 8th grade."

"After being in 8th grade for the second year, don't you think it'll serve you right to do your work so you can move on to the 9th grade and go to high school? I know your parents are wondering whether they should put you on meds or sign you up to see a shrink. Because if you keep this up, you're gonna be old enough to teach Driver's Ed."

#Zach, a Driver's Ed teacher? No way! I'd rather grow old in my parent's basement and eat Dillon's mother's cooking.

29

By JC Alexander

"Don't you worry about me, I've got my life mapped out." I assured Dillon.

While he and I chopped it up at his locker, our blonde beauty appeared out of nowhere. We couldn't believe our eyes. Walking along side of her was the 8th grade academic counselor, Mrs. Russell. And it became clear at that very moment that this hottie was off limits. "Are my eyes deceiving me? Or are we burnt toast?" Dillon commented.

I knew what he meant the moment he opened his mouth. Our blonde hottie was an 8th grader just like us. What a beautiful day!

"Dillon, will you show our new student Lauren where Mrs. Resnick's classroom is?"

"Sure." Dillon agreed.

"Mrs. Russell, how come you didn't ask me? You know I could find my way around this school blindfolded." I smiled. "And besides, I've been attending this school longer than anyone, so I can school her on all the do's and don'ts."

Mrs. Russell smiled. "Tell you what? Why don't you and Dillon both walk Lauren to her class."

"Roger that." I said.

"Take care of her you guys." She instructed us.

"Oh we will." I assured her.

While Dillon was grabbing a few books from his locker I gently grabbed Lauren by her hand and proceeded down the hallway towards Mrs. Resnick's class. "Let's carry on this way." I insisted.

"Hey shouldn't we wait for your friend?" she questioned me as she looked back at Dillon.

"Oh don't worry about him. He's gotta stick around and wait for his girlfriend." I told her and then I wrapped my arm around her shoulder.

By JC Alexander

#Gotta' show her who's the man around here!

"What school are you coming from?" I asked her. I lowered my voice to sound like I was an adult since I lacked in the height department.

"Princess Anne Middle School." She replied. I could tell she was a bit shy.

"Are you seeing anyone?" I didn't hesitate to ask.

"No," she told me.

Hearing that she didn't have a boyfriend made me want to do a back flip but I decided against it because I didn't want to come across like I was sweating her. Popular guys like me don't go around sweating girls. Girls sweat guys like me. It was the rule of thumb.

Immediately after Lauren and I arrived at the entryway of Mrs. Resnick's class, I cornered her

with the hopes that she'd give me her number so I'd be able to text her later and win the bet Dillon and I made yesterday.

#Operation "Scoop up the Hot Girl" was in full effect!

By JC Alexander

Chapter Five - Dillon

I watched as my best friend swooped in on Lauren like a hawk and carried her away. What was so hilarious about it was how he used the girl friend trick to pull Lauren away from me. No girl wants to hear that another girl is in the picture.

#And I clearly lost major points because of it.

I closed my locker and watched Zach as he made his move on Lauren. I looked at Zach's expression and I had to admit that he was looking awfully thirsty. I mean he was acting borderline stalker. And he was spreading it on very thick. But when he pointed to his newly cut Mohawk, I knew I had to step in.

I immediately took my iPhone from the front pocket of my shorts and held it out as I walked towards them. "Hey Zach, got your moms on the phone. She says she's at the supermarket and wants to know if you want her to pick you up a box of Huggies so you won't wet the bed tonight."

Lauren looked at Zach with the most disgusting expression she could muster up. "Oh my God! You wet the bed?" she blurted out and then she scrambled into her classroom.

"No, he's just kidding!" Zach tried to explain. But Lauren refused to look back.

I burst into laughter as I walked towards Zach. "Having girl problems lover boy?"

"Thanks a lot genius!" Zach said.

"Anytime my friend. Anytime." I replied.

After Lauren ran into Mrs. Resnick's classroom, Zach and I headed to our next class. It was second bell, which meant we had gym. Zach and I loved gym class. Mr. Fenster was our gym

teacher and he was the laziest guy ever. Zach and I practically ran the class ourselves while Mr. Fenster watched from the bleachers. He was more interested in searching profiles of women from online dating sites than instructing us on fitness.

"So did you get Lauren's number?" I chuckled while we changed into our gym clothes.

"How was I supposed to do that after you told her I wet the bed?

"The same way you got her away from me after you told her I was waiting for my girl friend."

Zach smiled. "Things we'd do to win a girl's heart. So may the best man win!" Zach said.

#Zach was so sure of himself. But I created the blueprint of "How to Win a Girl's Heart," so in my mind he'd forever be defeated.

Normally my mom would pick Zach and I up after school, but for some odd reason my dad showed up today. He refused to sit in the car like all the other parents did after they parked alongside the curb in front of the school. Instead he met Zach and I a few feet from the exit door of the school. "Hi you guys," ready to hang out with the big dawg?" he said. I couldn't believe how hip he was trying to sound. He also used

hand motions so he could look cool while he was talking.

#Talk about shear embarrassment. All the kids from my school turned around and looked straight at him. I swear I wanted to turn around and walk right back in school.

Conveniently Zach found my dad to be very funny. He cracked up with laughter. "Hey Dillon, think we can get your dad to take us to Hooters?"

I'm Just a Normal Kid

I punched Zach in his arm and stormed down the steps of the school. Zach followed with my dad in tow. "Hey, wait for me." Zach yelled.

As I approached my dad's car, I bumped into the new girl Lauren and accidently knocked her books out of her hands. I scrambled to pick her things up from the ground. I saw my dad through my peripheral vision as he stood on the sidelines. Zach stood there beside him with his arms folded like he was a freaking overseer or something. "I am so sorry." I apologized to her.

"It's okay." She said softly.

After I picked up her things and handed them to her she looked at me and smiled. "Hope your girl friend doesn't get jealous if she sees me talking to you." She commented.

"I don't have a girl friend. My friend only said that so he could get you to himself."

"Well, in that case, put my number in your phone and text me later." She insisted.

"Sure, I can do that." I told her.

By JC Alexander

After I programed her number into my iPhone, she walked off. I continued on to my dad's car. He and Zach joined me a few seconds later. "Son, you make me so proud." My dad commented as he patted me on my shoulders.

"Ahhh Mr. Carmichael that's so sweet of you to support Dillon on his dating efforts. But I'm the one who schools him on how to be cool. So remind me to have my secretary to forward you a bill for my services."

I ignored Zach's claims about how he taught me to be cool. I was more focused on what I would say to Lauren later when I start texting her.

Chapter Six - Zach

My brother Matt and his friends were all huddled around his laptop drooling over Dillon's sister Julie again. Like clockwork she logged onto Skype and performed in her birthday suit for everyone to see. Usually I'd be hiding underneath my brother's bed. But since I was helping my mom put away the groceries she had just bought in from the supermarket I lost track of time and I settled for the next best thing, and that was a nosebleed seat at my brother's bedroom door with it slightly ajar.

#What's wrong if I wanna get a sneak peak too?

By JC Alexander

Three minutes into the show my knees started aching. It felt like I had the knees of a sixty-five-year-old man. So, while I was trying to find a better seating position my mother snuck up behind me and blew my cover. "Zach what are you doing peaking into your brother's room?" she asked.

#My mother was a divorce attorney so she questioned every move anyone in our family made.

I stood up on my feet while my brother and his friends all turned around to see what was going on. "Matt, it looks like your little brother is a perve!" one of his friends said and chuckled.

I'm Just a Normal Kid

My mom pushed my brother's bedroom door open. "Matt what is going on in here? And why is Zach peaking into your room? She asked.

My brother Matt minimized the Skype window on his laptop before our mother saw what we were watching. "Mom, I don't know. Ask him." Matt insisted.

My mother turned towards me. As a matter of fact, everyone including my brother Matt turned their attention towards me. It felt like I was in the hot seat. And it wasn't a good feeling at all.

I thought for a moment because I knew I couldn't blow the whistle on Matt. He'd kill me. So, I made up a lie about how I was eavesdropping on Matt and his friends' conversation about how they hook up with girls. Unfortunately for me, my mother didn't buy it. She knew I didn't respect Matt or his friends for that matter. And she knew I thought his pick-up lines to girls were whack and corny.

By JC Alexander

She stood there with her arms folded so I dug back into my bag of lies and came up with something far more convincing. "Okay, the real reason why I was peaking into Matt's room was because I was going to play a prank on them."

My mom looked at me and then she turned and looked at Matt. I knew it was hard for her to believe anything that came out of my mouth. But she was gonna have to take one for the team this time. "All right, you guys. You better behave. And Matt you need to clean up this room. It looks like you're sleeping in a land field " She commented and then she left.

"Okay, mom." Matt said.

Soon after our mother left, Matt and his friends gave me the evil eye. "You know if you would've blown my cover I would've killed you right?" Matt warned me.

"Let's just say you owe me one." I smiled.

Matt knew I had a smoking gun. So, he'd better tread lightly or he's going down.

#It isn't fun when the rabbit got the gun!

Matt and his friends logged back onto Julie's peep show. But I was ejected from the room and he even locked the door after my departure. Talk about a major let down.

By JC Alexander

Chapter Seven – Dillon

I sent Lauren my first text around eight o'clock. I asked her how old she was and she told me she was thirteen. Then I asked her had she ever had a boy friend? And she told me she did. She also told me that he attended her old middle school and that they broke up because she told him that she and her parents were moving.

"Have u eva kissed a guy b4?" I text.

"Of course silly!" she answered. "Wat about u?" she asked me.

I'd kissed a ton of girls. But I figured if I told Lauren that, she'd think I was a chick magnet. But then I figured if I told her that I hadn't then she'd think that I was a loser! So in the end I went with my better judgment and told her the truth.

"Yea I kissed a few girls." I finally text.

"Oh really?

"Yea really." I assured her.

We continued to make small talk. I told her about the skate park Zach and I hang out at. And then I filled her in about the popular and the not so popular kids at school. I could tell right from the start that she was interested in being a part of the popular club. So, I told her I'd introduce her to kids in my circle while we're in school tomorrow. Every boy and girl in our clique was popular and she'd definitely fit in. "Would u introduce me as your new girlfriend?" she asked me.

"Sure," I replied. My heart skipped a couple beats. I couldn't believe that I had just gotten a new girlfriend and I hadn't even asked her out.

#Want to be cool like me? Call 555-1234.

By JC Alexander

While Lauren and I text back and forth I was getting used to the idea that she was my new girl-friend. Boy was Zach going to be devastated when he got wind of this! I figured now would be a good time to get all of my homework assignments in order.

"Dillon it's time to eat dinner honey," my mother yelled as she knocked on my bedroom door.

"Okay, I'll be down in a minute." I told her.

#As much as I'd rather skip dinner, I knew it would hurt my mother's feelings. So, remind me to call and have a paramedic on standby before I take my first bite.

A couple of minutes later Lauren and I ended our texting session. I told her it was dinnertime and that it was my mother's turn to destroy what white blood cells we had left in our body.

In other words, I told her I'd text her back if I made it out of the kitchen alive.

Lauren found what I said to be funny. But I was serious. And if she had to endure my mother's cooking on a regular, she'd know exactly what I was talking about.

By JC Alexander

Chapter Eight - Zach

From the moment Dillon's mother picked me up this morning and until the time she dropped Dillon and I off to school, Dillon poured on the details of his texts with Lauren really thick. And when he told me that she wanted him to introduce her to our clique in school as his girlfriend, I knew I had been bamboozled.

"Seriously dude, you just ruined my chances of ever having Lauren and I to become one." I finally commented after we exited Dillon's mother's car.

"Oh get over it. You're acting like I broke up your marriage engagement."

"Well that was what I was gunning for." I replied while we approached the front entrance of our school.

I'm Just a Normal Kid

The schoolyard was filled with all the kids that attended our school. On one side there stood a group of the rockers. They dressed in all black with spiked accessories and they listened to heavy rock music. The next group of kids was the geek squad. Not all of them wore glasses but they acted the part. And they had excellent test scores to prove it.

#Unbeknownst to my parents, I've paid for a few homework assignments. I figured it was better to cheat than to fail.

51

By JC Alexander

Last but certainly not least was the group of kids Dillon and I hung out with. We were definitely the popular kids. We had the look; the swag and we had the not-so-popular kids wanting to be like us. What a great position to be in?

The only downside to being me right now was the fact that Dillon won the bet. How was I able to come back from that? Lauren was literally the hottest girl in school right now and I didn't have her. What a freaking bummer?

After Dillon and I met up with our other friends, Lauren approached us from behind. "Hi Dillon," she smiled.

Dillon and I both turned around. Well actually, everybody in our circle turned around. Lauren was so freaking hot and I was literally kicking myself in the butt for losing the bet to Dillon.

"Hey Lauren, what's up?" he said. And then he introduced her to everyone in our huddle as his girlfriend.

 52

"Wow, it's been less than twenty-four hours and you guys are already going steady? Talk about a cheap date!" I said.

#Now that I think about it, Dillon hadn't spent one red cent on her. I guess you can actually get the milk without buying the cow!

Dillon smacked me across the head. "Cut it out Zach." He said, clinching his teeth.

"Hold on to your pants Casanova. I was only kidding!" I replied.

"You're such a jerk!" Lauren said.

"Tell me something I don't know." I told her.

Before Lauren could come back with some girly remark, the school bell rang. "I guess that 's our cue." I said aloud.

"Thank God!" Dillon said as he walked towards the entrance of the school with Lauren in tow.

Chapter Nine – Dillon

The lunchroom was the place where everyone migrated to hang out with their friends. It was a place where we could goof off and not be held accountable for our actions.

#Only half of us ate lunch while the other half swapped test answers or conjured up schemes to sabotage a substitute teacher's plans to teach our class.

By JC Alexander

I stood in line to get two slices of pizza when Megan walked up behind me. "Would you hand me a carton of chocolate milk?" she asked me.

"Sure," I said. And handed her the milk she asked for.

She held her head down a little. I assumed she did this to avoid looking at me head on. There was no denying how shy she was. And when she finally said thank you, I realized that my assumption was true. "Why don't you ever look at me when we talk to each other?"

"It's just a force of habit," she replied. She looked at me for a half of a second and then she lowered her head once again.

I wasn't the type of guy that took an interest in girls from another social circle and especially a girl from the geek squad. But for some odd reason I was attracted to Megan. I couldn't figure out if it was because she was shy or nice.

After I paid the cafeteria cashier I headed to my usual table. Megan proceeded to the other

side of the lunchroom. I wanted to ask her to join me at my table but I knew that was forbidden.

#My friends would've freaked out and voted me out of the club, so I threw caution to the wind.

One by one all of my friends joined me at the lunch table. Zach came later than usual. And when he sat down at the table I asked him where he'd been? "Mrs. Saunders made me sit in her class for an extra fifteen minutes because she thought that I deliberately interrupted her class when I passed gas." Zach explained.

"Come on Zach, really?"

"Hey what was I supposed to do? Hold it?"

"Yeah why not?"

"Hey, my dad is good friends with our family doctor and I've personally heard him say that you can die if you hold gas inside of you."

Everyone at the table burst into laughter. "Ewwww, Zach we're going to start calling you fart boy."

"Oh whatever you guys! You would've done the same thing to." Zach said after he took a huge bite of his pizza. He talked while he chewed the entire slice. And the funny part about it was that Zach was being himself.

"Hey Dillon, where's your new girlfriend?" Zach blurted out. "Hey you guys, did Dillon tell you how he stole the new girl right from under me?" Zach continued as he looked at everyone at the lunch table. He wanted an audience and he got one.

"Cut it out Zach! You know I won that bet fair and square." I spoke up.

#Lauren was totally screaming to be with a hot guy. And I was her only hope.

"Don't forget I almost had her eating out of my hands until he lied on me." Zach pointed out.

"Oh get over it lover boy! You lost so deal with it." I chuckled.

By JC Alexander

Chapter Ten - Zach

#It's a known fact that I didn't need lessons on how to be a butt hole. I was born this way.

But in the case of Dillon versus Lauren, he totally blindsided me. I didn't have a shot at her from the moment she and her parents moved into the neighborhood. So in other words, this calls for a do over. And I made Dillon painfully aware of that while we were on our way to the skate park. "You didn't tell Lauren you were going to be at the skate park did you?" I asked him.

"No I didn't. But why do you ask?

"You know I deserve a do over, right?"

"You mean a do over with the bet we made about Lauren?"

"Yeah, that would be accurate."

Dillon burst into laughter. Come on dude, you can't be serious. I won that bet fair and square."

"Well, how come I feel flimflammed?"

"Believe me, it's a figment of your imagination. And it's totally acceptable given the fact that you've been in the eighth grade twice already."

"Quit it with the eighth grade jokes. I have you to know that I'm a fairly intelligent guy. I just act like I'm dumb."

"Go figure." Dillon laughed once more.

"You can laugh all you want lover boy. But one of these days I'm gonna defeat you in every bet we make and I'm gonna wear the crown with dignity and honor."

"Dignity and honor. Sounds like you've been watching too many shows on the Nickelodeon channel."

"Don't worry about what kind of show I watch. You just worry about how badly I'm about to make you look after I show you my new freestyle moves on the half pipe." I told him.

#I figured if I couldn't beat him at getting hot girls, then I'd better beat him at skateboarding.

Chapter Eleven - Dillon

Lauren and I have been going steady for a couple of weeks now. She's become Zach's friend now too. It took a little persuading on my part but she finally gave in. Now we're one big happy family.

Speaking of family, my sister Julie and her nagging best friend Molly started busting my chops when they saw me standing outside the house talking to Megan. I was actually fixing the back rim of her bike. But it didn't matter to them. "Owww…I'm telling Lauren you're cheating on her!" Julie yelled from the front door.

"Yeah, I'm telling too." Molly yelled.

"Don't you guys have a laptop to undress in front of?" I yelled back at them.

By JC Alexander

#Those two were really getting on my nerves. So, I had to hit them where it hurts.

"Oh screw you!" Julie yelled. And then she slammed the door shut.

I continued fixing Megan's bike. And what do you know Lauren pulls up in the car with her mother. Lauren had cheerleading practice earlier in the day so it made sense that she'd be coming home around this time.

It didn't take long for her to get out of the car. And as soon as I heard the car door close she stormed in our direction. With both of her hands folded against her chest she started asking me fifty questions. "What are you doing?"

"I'm fixing her bike rim." I explained.

"I see that. But why are you doing it?"

"Because I offered to do it."

"Why can't she get her own boyfriend to do it?"

"Maybe because she doesn't have one."

"So, it's our fault that she doesn't have a boyfriend?"

"Come on Lauren. Do we really have to do this now?"

"It's okay. I can get my dad to fix it." Megan insisted and then she grabbed ahold of the handlebars.

"Yes, please get your dad to fix it." Lauren told her.

Without any hesitation Megan pulled her bike from my grip and pushed it back in the direction of her house. I felt so bad for her.

By JC Alexander

#I guess I just experienced a day in the life of a nerd and it wasn't pretty!

After Megan headed home I stood there trying to figure out how I was going to apologize for the way Lauren treated her. I mean it wasn't like I encouraged it. So, maybe she'd give me a chance to make things right with her.

Before I went into the house Lauren grilled me about my affiliation with Megan. "I can't believe that you were seriously trying to fix her bike."

"Is it because she's not popular?"

"Exactly." Lauren said as if she was proving a point.

But I didn't agree with her. Megan was a nice girl. So she deserved to be treated nicely. Too

bad my friends wouldn't see what I saw in her. Who knows maybe one day they would.

#The way Lauren carried on about Megan made me realize how badly the not-so-popular kids were being treated.

After Lauren ragged on me like an old lady she went home. And boy was I glad of that. I swear I never knew that having a girlfriend could be so much work.

#Guess I'm just a normal kid with girl problems!

67

Chapter Twelve - Zach

"Mom I need ten bucks for my lunch account." I yelled from the kitchen. I was on my way out of the house to go to school but realized that I needed lunch money and since my dad had already left for work I knew I had to get it from my mother.

"Zach, I thought your dad gave you enough lunch money to last you this entire month?" she replied as she joined me in the kitchen.

"He did but somehow or another I over spent on days where I wanted to grab extra snacks." I explained.

"Zach stop it with the lies. You and I both know about this unorthodox habit you have. Now we won't call it gambling because it sounds so harsh. But we will acknowledge the fact that that word exists and that your father and I will

find you the best doctor out there so they can help you in that area."

"Really mom?" I blurted out.

#In my mind, she was truly overreacting. Which brings me to the point that drama queens come in all ages!

"Of course darling. Your father and I won't see it any other way."

"What about my lunch money? Do I have to go and see a doctor for that too?" I asked sarcastically. I wasn't in the mood to hear all the mumbo jumbo about the bets I make in school with my lunch money. All I wanted was a few

bucks to get me through the rest of the week. Was that too much to ask for?

Finally after several more agonizing minutes of verbal torture my mother handed me the ten bucks I asked for. And on my way out of the house I wondered how much longer I would've had to stay on lock and key if I had asked her for her keys to her BMW?

#Parents have no concept of how valuable our time is. We're always going nowhere fast.

Chapter Thirteen - Dillon

Zach and the rest of our buddies from school asked me to meet them at the skate park but I declined the offer and told them I had to help my parents out with a few things around the house. The truth of the matter was that I had promised to fix Megan's bike rim. So that's what I intended to do.

I skated down to her house and when I got there she took me into her parent's garage where her bike was. "I appreciate you coming down here to fix my bike." She said.

I noticed she always held her head down when she talked to me.

I grabbed the bottom of her chin to lift up her head but she pushed my hand away and turned her head away from me. "Why do you always

look away from me when I try to talk to you?" I asked her.

She pushed her glasses back on her nose and said, "Why does it matter if I look at you?"

I chuckled to make light of the situation. "Because it's the polite thing to do." I reasoned with her.

"I think your girlfriend needs more help in that department than me."

"I think you're right." I agreed.

#Lauren was an evil villain. And she made Freddy Kruger look like the tooth fairy!

I couldn't believe how long it took me to get Megan to let her guard down. I expressed to her

that I was a good guy even though I was very popular around school. "Too bad we can't say the same about your girlfriend." She commented.

I smiled. "I can't speak for her. I can only speak for myself." I replied.

Megan and I continued to kick it while I worked on her bike rim. And before we knew it an hour had passed. We laughed and talked about teachers we hated and the ones who dressed funny. It really felt good to be myself. And I'm sure Megan felt the same way. In fact, before I left her parent's garage I gave her a hug and told her to text me whenever she wanted to talk.

Before I went to bed Megan text me and thanked me again for fixing her bike. She even expressed how much of an awesome time she had with me.

By JC Alexander

I wanted to text her back and tell her I had an even more awesome time with her but guys don't do that. It's lame to show more enthusiasm than a girl. I learned that rule in third grade.

The next day in school Zach and I walked by Megan's locker while she was standing there talking to one of her friends. I smiled at her and she smiled back. Her friend whispered something to Megan and then she giggled. I thought it was cute. But Zach didn't.

"What are you geeks smiling at?" he blurted out.

I smacked him in the back of the head with my binder. "Come on dude, leave 'em alone." I told him.

By JC Alexander

Chapter Fourteen - Zach

My brother Matt and his friends were up to their same old tricks. All of his high school buddies congregated in his bedroom to get their daily dose of Dillon's sister Julie. But make no mistake I was there too. I beat everyone in the room and found my place underneath my brother's bed. Unfortunately though, my time down there was short lived.

#The smell and infestation of Matt's sweaty jockey straps and dirty boxer shorts nearly had me hyperventilating and I had to run for cover.

As the striptease started I was scrambling to get from underneath the bed. My sudden movement startled everyone in the room but I could care less. It was either my life or their mental state of mind. And I picked my life of course.

#I figured those wanna-be football players would come out of this all right. Me scaring them was only a minor bump in the road.

"Zach, what's with you sneaking in my room?" My brother Matt asked. He looked shocked to see me.

"Dude, I told you your brother was a perve." The same guy commented again.

By JC Alexander

I stood up from the floor and stood in front of everyone. I flexed my muscles to let these chumps know that I wasn't a perve. I was more of a man than they'd ever be.

I looked at Matt's friend first and said, "First of all I'm not a perve, you enbesol." And then I turned my focus on Matt. "If you would've cleaned underneath your bed you would not have known I was even in here." I tried to rationalize.

#Never take the fall even when you get caught red handed. And always shift the blame. That tactic seems to work mostly with my dad.

Too bad it didn't work in this situation. Matt grabbed me by the back of my t-shirt and escorted me out of his room quicker than I could say *Hell Mary*.

#Since Dillon was at home doing his homework and I had nowhere else to go, I figured it may not be such a bad idea if I did my own homework. I mean it's not like I could lose cool points for doing it. Smart kids do it all the time, right?

By JC Alexander

Chapter Fifteen - Dillon

My mother invited Lauren and her parents over to eat dinner with us tonight. It was my mother's way of showing them how neighborly she was. My dad and I tried to talk her out of having them over up until the minute our doorbell rang, but she wouldn't listen. Thankfully though, Lauren's mother brought over a dish of her own. She baked some weird looking casserole. So, my dad used this opportunity to redirect the attention from my mother's pot roast to Lauren's mother's dish. This was the first time my dad had ever used his brain! Good for you dad!

Once plan B was set into motion and my mother's cooking was safely put away in a secured location of our house, everyone sat down at the dining room table. In the beginning it felt a little awkward for me to sit at the table and eat

dinner with my girlfriend's parents. To be candid, the mood was completely dead.

#I figured I could liven up the place if I burped or farted!

Luckily for our parents Lauren lied about having to use the bathroom because I got up and offered to show her where it was. If she had not done that, I would've gassed up the whole room real good.

"I really don't have to use the bathroom," she confessed.

I smiled. "I kind of figured that," I said. "Come on, let's go into the family room and watch some TV." I suggested. Lauren and I went into the family room and sat down on the sofa.

By JC Alexander

"Wanna watch a movie or something?" I asked her.

"I don't care what we watch. I'm just glad that we're not in the same room with our parents anymore."

I let out a loud sigh. "Tell me about it." I commented. I picked up the remote control from the coffee table and sifted through the channels. After sifting through over fifty channels I stopped at the movie called *17 Again*.

Lauren and I laughed pretty much during the entire movie but all of that came to a screeching halt when I got a text from Megan. My iPhone was laying face up on the coffee table so it was very easy to see the name of the sender. So when Lauren saw Megan's name I had a lot of questions to answer.

She picked the phone up and read the message. "Why is she asking you are you busy?" Lauren wanted to know.

I took my phone from her hand. "It's nothing. She probably needs me to take another look at her bike." I lied. I really didn't know what to say. So, lying seemed to work better in this situation.

"So, you two are cool now?"

"No we're not."

"So, why does she want to know if you're busy?"

"What else do you want me to say? I already told you that she might be texting me because she wants me to take another look at her bike."

"Well, since you two aren't cool then text her and tell her to get lost." Lauren demanded. She folded her arms like she normally does when she's trying to get her way.

By JC Alexander

#Something told me that Lauren was going to crash this party. She was becoming this uncontrollable pre-Madonna and my dad never schooled me on how to handle those types of girls. Now that I think about it, he's only been with my mother and she's a total push over. So it looks like I'm screwed!

"Hey listen Lauren, Megan's a nice girl." I began to say. But she cut me off.

"I don't care how nice she is. She doesn't need to be texting you. I'm your girlfriend not her."

"Can we just talk about this later?" I asked her. I was feeling pressured to do something I didn't want to.

"No we can't. And if you don't do it then I'm going home." she told me. She was adamant too.

#I'm a 13-year-old kid. Is this what being married feels like? If it is, then I'll pass!

"Well Lauren, if you wanna leave and go home then so be it." I told her.

"Fine then," she said and stood up from the sofa.

85

By JC Alexander

#Like an overworked nanny getting socked in the nose by a bratty 5-year-old kid, Lauren stormed out of my house and I was happier than a kid in the candy store.

  86

Chapter Sixteen - Zach

"Dude what's up? You look like a dog with his tail between his legs." I commented when I entered into his bedroom. Dillon was lying on his bed watching *Sanjay and Craig* on the Nickelodeon channel.

"I think Lauren and I broke up."

I smiled and took a seat at the foot of his bed. "Really? That's awesome. Give me her number so I can call her and tell her that daddy is coming home." I replied.

"Seriously dude." Dillon said.

He didn't find what I said funny. "Come on dude, you can't blame me for trying. Remember I'm the only popular guy left in school that doesn't have a girlfriend." I told him.

"Do you have an off switch?" Dillon asked. I could tell he was getting irritated.

By JC Alexander

"My bad dude. Don't be so sensitive." I said.

"Try having a girlfriend that nags you like an old lady and see how you feel." Dillon told me.

"What happened?"

"She totally bugged out when that girl Megan texted my phone earlier."

"Are you talking about that geek that lives down the block and wears those huge, black swimming goggles?"

"Come on dude, lay off her glasses. Megan is a nice girl." Dillon defended her.

#It was super weird hearing my best friend take up for a girl that no one in school even knew exists. I'm thinking that maybe his parents need to do an

intervention on him. He's showing all the signs of a kid sniffing glue because popular guys aren't supposed to like, date or even feel sorry for geeky girls. He's totally violating all the rules mandated by us popular guys.

"Okay wait a minute, it sounds like you're taking on a charity case here."

"Megan isn't a charity case. She's a cool girl and I don't think anyone should be mean to her because she's not popular."

By JC Alexander

"So, what exactly are you saying?" I probed a little more. I needed some clarity as to where this conversation was going. And even though I rarely do my classwork, I have listened to my History teacher from time to time. So I remembered when she told the class that it was never a good idea to assume anything. Always ask questions she said. So, I figured that this would be the perfect opportunity to practice that exercise.

"I'm not saying anything. Let's just play a game of Mortal Kombat." He changed the subject.

Chapter Seventeen – Dillon

I thought that when I saw Lauren in school today she'd apologize to me for acting like a spoiled brat yesterday but she didn't. I couldn't believe how she and several of the cheerleaders from school walked by my locker as if Zach and I weren't standing there. She literally gave me the cold shoulders.

"Wow dude, she's really mad at you." he commented after he witnessed Lauren's actions.

I closed my locker and turned away from the direction that Laruen was walking and headed to my next class. Zach followed me because his next class was across the hall from mine.

"Who cares? She's being a total snob."

"First off, you're being a total wimp. What you need to do is be a little more aggressive like

the gangsters in the movies. Show her who the man is."

"You watch too much TV."

"You better listen to me. I've never been wrong about these things." Zach suggested.

"And when did you become a relationship guru?"

"Right after you stole her from underneath my nose, which is probably the reason you're having such a hard time with her. She and I wouldn't be having these problems if we were together." Zach replied hypothetically.

"Don't you have a test to flunk?" I replied sarcastically.

#I swear I was about to tell Zach that he could have Lauren and take her to where the sun doesn't shine. But I held my tongue and decided that I would handle this minor set back another way.

"Dude why don't you calm down. You know I'm just busting your chops." Zach joked.

"Will it kill you to get a life?"

"I'm not sure. Maybe I should try that." He chuckled. Zach was getting a big kick out of seeing me sulk behind Lauren's antics.

93

By JC Alexander

"Ha...Ha...Ha...! Laugh all you want." I said. I told him and then I turned and walked into my next class.

"Come on Dillon, lighten up. It's not the end of the world." I heard Zach shout from behind. His class was directly across from my class so it didn't take much for me to hear every word he had to say.

After the bell rang everyone took their seats and waited for the teacher to discuss our lesson for the day. I watched her as she gathered the papers together from her desk. And while this was going on someone dropped a tightly folded note on my desk. I immediately looked up to see who had dropped the note. To my surprise it was Megan. I was so worked up about the drama involving Lauren that I forgot Megan was in this class with me.

I looked around the classroom to make sure no one saw her drop the note on my desk. And

when I realized that the coast was clear I opened up the note and read it.

Dillon,

I appreciate you being my friend. It means the world to me. But I'm also sorry that you and Lauren broke up because of me. If there's anything I can do to make it right, I'm here for you.

Sincerely,

Megan.

By JC Alexander

As soon as I finished reading Megan's note I folded it back up and slid it in my shirt pocket. Now wasn't a good time to thank her for the note. I figured I'd be able to get her to myself later in the day before school let out. That way no one sees us talking.

Chapter Eighteen - Zach

I ran out of the class to meet Dillon in the hallway since our classes were across from one another. Before our classes began he was feeling a little down and out so I thought of a way to boost up his spirits and I wanted to share it with him.

"Hey dude, I've got the perfect thing to cheer you up." I said when I approached him.

Dillon sighed. "What is it now?" he asked me.

But before I could tell him about my perfect plan, we noticed that there was a poster hanging up on the wall next to our classes that wasn't there earlier. All the kids standing in the hallway were huddled in a circle reading it. So, Dillon and I walked over and looked at it ourselves and it read:

By JC Alexander

This year's school Halloween costume dance will be held inside the gymnasium

on OCTOBER 30th

from 6 to 8pm

Tickets can be purchased from your homeroom teacher

Don't forget to wear your best costume!

"Oh yeah, looks like I'm about to get my mack on. I'm gonna have all the girls begging me to take them to this dance." I said.

"Well, have fun." Dillon commented.

"Wait a minute, you're not going?" I asked.

"For what? My girlfriend is acting all weird," he replied.

"You're acting like it's the end of the world. Look at all of these beautiful girls in our midst. Just pick one of them and call it a day." I advised him.

See I was relationship specialist. I knew what it took to get a hot girl and I knew what it took to keep her. My buddy Dillon was too occupied to think about anything outside of Lauren. But I figured as long as he had me holding him down, he'd be back on his A-game by the end of the school year.

By JC Alexander

Chapter Nineteen - Dillon

Zach and I were sitting at the lunchroom table eating our lunch with a couple of friends when a fight broke out. I was stuffing my face with a hot dog when the commotion started. "If you don't stay away from Dillon I'm gonna make your life so miserable." I heard a girl's voice yell. And when I saw that the girl yelling was Lauren I was shocked.

"Dude, your girlfriend is ripping that geeky girl to shreds over there?" Zach said.

In disbelief, I stood up to my feet. "Dude, what is her problem?" I spoke out. I felt so sorry for Megan as I stood there while Lauren scolded her like she was a kid or something.

"Dillon you might want to go over there and get `that situation under control." My other buddy suggested.

 100

"Yeah dude, you better break that up before it gets messier than it already is." Zach added.

At the advice of my friends I walked over to the other side of the cafeteria to break up the fight between Lauren and Megan. Well in all honesty, it really wasn't a fight. Lauren was taunting Megan like a bully. Megan held her head down the entire time. "Lauren what's your problem?" I interjected as I stood between them.

"She's the problem. So, tell her to stop texting you and lose your number." Lauren spat.

"Lauren you are really bugging me out right now." I told Lauren. And then I turned my attention to Megan. "Megan, go to a table and eat your food." I instructed her.

"So, you're not gonna tell her to stop texting you?" Lauren continued. She was causing a huge commotion. Everyone in the lunchroom watched her in action.

"Dude, chill why don't you?" I instructed Lauren and then I turned and faced Megan, who

was looking frazzled as she held on to her lunch tray. "Go sit down and eat your food." I said to her. I felt like I needed to deal with Lauren first.

"Oh so, you're really not gonna tell her to stop texting, huh?" Lauren pressed the issue.

Before I could make any attempt to calm Lauren down all three male cafeteria monitors who were also hallway monitors busted our little circle up. One by one they broke up the crowd and sent all of us to our tables. "You guys know we don't tolerate this kind of behavior." One of the monitors said.

All of the kids standing around walked away and returned to their tables. Lauren and her newfound friends returned to their table as well. Zach and I watched Lauren and her friends as they laughed and made wise cracks about Megan. And when I looked to see what Megan was doing while Lauren and her friends were acting out, she was gone. I searched the entire lunchroom and

she was nowhere to be found. I figured she dumped her lunch in the trash and left.

At the lunch table all of my buddies had something to say, including Zach. "Dillon how does it feel to have girls fighting over you?" Zach spoke first.

"Yeah Dillon, you're the man!" another friend commented.

"That wasn't cool you guys. Lauren was bullying her."

"Lauren is the hottest girl in this entire school. So, in my eyes she can't do no wrong." Zach said.

"Is that all you think about?" I asked Zach.

"Face it dude. You got a hottie so she gets a free pass." Zach replied.

"You guys are pathetic." I told them.

By JC Alexander

#If a scoop of stupid was served on an ice cream cone, Zach and my other buddies would be the first in line.

Zach and I headed to our next class after our lunch period was over. "How long are you and Lauren not going to talk to each other?" Zach wanted to know.

"Why do you care?" I asked.

"Can I be concerned about the welfare of my best friend?" Zach smiled.

"I'm fine Dr. Phil."

Chapter Twenty - Zach

My fifth bell Science teacher sent me to the office with a referral notice alleging that I was becoming a nuisance in class. I wasn't becoming anything. I asked her several times if I could go to the bathroom but she said no.

#So, why say I was a nuisance because I had to fart? I only did it three times.

En route to the principal's office I saw the geeky girl Megan coming out of the girl's bath-room. She was alone so I used this time to con-

front her about my buddy Dillon. I walked up to her and said, "Hey Megan, mind if I talk to you for a minute?"

"You wanna talk to me?" she asked. Nerdy chicks never get the chance to be in the company of popular guys like me so I could tell how surprised she was that I even approached her.

"Yeah, I do." I replied.

"About what?" she wanted to know. She was very nervous.

"I wanna know what's up with you and Dillon?"

"There's nothing going on between us."

"I don't believe you."

"No. I'm being totally honest. Nothing is going on. He fixed my bike the other day and that was it," she explained.

"Well, I'm glad that you aren't expecting anything else because I know what type of girls he likes and you aren't his type."

"His girlfriend Lauren has already made me aware of that." She said and then she looked back down towards the floor.

"Good. Well, I'm glad that we're all on the same page." I responded.

"If you're done then I'm gonna leave and go back to my class." She said.

"Yeah, you do that." I insisted and then I walked away.

Mr. Carson, the school's principal was waiting with bated breath when I walked into his office. "Have a seat Zach," he said as soon as he laid eyes on me. He sat behind his desk like he was the head honcho at some huge company. If he thought he was intimidating me then he was delusional. Nothing about Mr. Carson was intimidating. All the kids at this school look at Mr. Carson as a weirdo because he was so goofy looking.

By JC Alexander

#What Mr. Carson needed to do was grow some hair on his chest because he was one wimpy adult.

Aside from that, the guy was tall, very skinny, and he dressed like his clothes came from the swap meet. He was in serious need of some lessons on what and what not to wear in public.

After I took a seat in front of his desk he said, "So young man, your teacher tells me that you were disrupting her classroom."

"That's not what I was doing." I blurted out.

"So, tell me what you were doing?" he wanted me to explain.

"All I can say is that I raised my hand and asked if I could go to the bathroom and when I was told no, I went to plan b."

"Which was?"

"Come on Mr. Carson, we're both men. You know where I am going with this." I smiled.

"Oh really?"

I smiled again. "Yes sir. I feel that as a man, it's important that I don't let anything pollute my body. And if I can't pass gas when I needed to then I'd be doing just that."

"Thank you for that medical update."

"No problem. I'm here anytime you need me." I assured him.

He looked at me like I'd lost my mind. But everyone looks at me that way so his actions weren't anything out of the ordinary.

"Listen Zach, I understand you had issues passing gas so the next time you have another one of those episodes, please excuse yourself from the class and if your teacher has a problem with it then you come see me. Got it?"

"Yes sir, I got it." I smiled.

 109

By JC Alexander

On my way out of Mr. Carson's office, I left him with a gift and farted as loud as I could. The gas from my butt sounded like a trumpet. Brrrrrrrrrrrrrrrrkkkkkkk!

#I'm sure Mr. Carson thought my fart sounded atrocious. But I'm sure he found it to smell even worse.

Chapter Twenty-One - Dillon

"Dillon I need you to take out the trash darling." My mother yelled from the kitchen.

I was in the den area of the house with my dad when I heard my mother calling my name. "I'm in the family room talking to dad so give me a second," I yelled back.

"Okay." She yelled back.

My dad literally had me under lock and key with this big idea that he had to school me on how to keep a girlfriend. He knew there was trouble in paradise after noticing that Lauren hadn't been over to our house in a few days. When he first asked me how things were going with she and I, I lied and told him we were cool. But he knew something was wrong, that's why he sat me down to talk. "Son, you've got to show girls that they matter. And if you have to

carry their books for them everyday then do it. Girls like it when you take control." He said.

I knew my dad meant well but because he had no idea what he was talking about. Not only that, I refused to accept relationship advice from a dude who wears permanent creases in his pants. That's fashion suicide in and of itself.

"Dad, I thank you for giving me all the girl advice but I believe I can handle things from here." I assured him.

"I know you know what you're doing son, but you can never know too much about girls."

"I'm feeling you dad. But, I've got things under control. Lauren and I only had a little disagreement. She'll be back in my arms by the end of school tomorrow." I insisted.

"Okay. Well, just remember that I'm here when you need to talk."

"Thanks dad,"

"No problem son."

Immediately after I left my dad's presence I hauled butt to the kitchen to help my mother with trash duty. I hated taking out the trash but it looked so appealing today.

I was at the point where I'd wiped my sister's butt after she did the number two before I'd sit there and listen to my dad talk. He was that annoying.

It took me no time to dump the trash for my mother. I was outside and back in the house in less than twenty seconds flat. On my way back into my bedroom I bumped into my sister Julie again. She had just come out of the bathroom. "I

113

heard dad giving you girlfriend advice." She smiled.

I tried to walk by her so I could get to my bedroom. "And so what?" I commented.

"I figured you must be terribly desperate to sit down and talk to dad about your girlfriend across the street."

"It's really funny how you mention the word desperate when I hear you take your clothes off and dance topless in front of your computer everyday just so you can boost up your numbers to become the next homecoming queen."

Julie's face turned red that instant. I knew I had hit her right below the belt and I loved it. There was nothing like victory. "Now if you don't mind, I'd like to get by so I can go to my room." I continued.

Frozen solid, Julie just stood there with her mouth wide open. So, immediately after I walked by her I looked back and said, "Close

I'm Just a Normal Kid

your mouth before you catch something you won't be able to get rid of."

By JC Alexander

Chapter Twenty-Two - Zach

"Is there anything I can help you fellows with?" the store clerk asked Dillon and I. We only had a few days left until the school's costume dance so we headed to the mall to pick out our Halloween costumes.

"No, we're good. But thank you anyway." I told the lady.

"Don't mention it you guys."

Dillon and I walked up and down the aisles in the store and finally found a few costumes that we could choose from. "Hey Dillon, take a look at this one." I said as I held up a Halloween costume of Wolverine.

"Yeah, that's cool. I can see all the girls in school throwing themselves at you." Dillon said.

"I am irresistible, huh?" I smiled.

"Yeah, you sure are lover boy. Gabriella isn't gonna be able to keep her hands off you." Dillon joked.

"You love busting my chops."

Dillon laughed. "Better me than Gabriella, right?"

Dillon knew I hated being reminded about Gabriella and I making out. No one was supposed to find out about that. Gabriella and I were supposed to be a secret. I had never kissed a girl before so I practiced on her so I'd be ready for the real thing when it happened. But now everyone in school knows what happened and every once in a while I'd get reminded about it. Thank God Gabriella doesn't attend our school anymore because if she did, I'd be reminded about our incident on a daily basis.

"Knock it off and find your costume so we can get out of here." I replied.

By JC Alexander

After sifting through several costumes, Dillon finally decided on an Iron man costume. "Whatcha' think? Is this okay?" he asked me.

"Yeah, it's pretty cool. But what is Lauren going to the dance as?" I wanted to know.

"I don't know."

"Whatcha' mean you don't know?"

"I didn't ask her."

"So, you guys still haven't talked?"

"Nope."

"Well aren't you taking her to the dance?"

"I'm not sure."

"Well have you at least talked to her about it?"

"Nope."

"Sounds to me like you're going to the dance alone."

"You might be right." He said as he picked out an Iron Man costume. "Let's get out of here." He continued and then he walked off and

headed to the counter where the store clerk was to pay for his costume.

By JC Alexander

Chapter Twenty-Three – Dillon

Once Zach and I paid for our Halloween costumes we parted ways. I went home and so did he. Several minutes after I dropped my Halloween costume onto my bed my iPhone rang. I grabbed it from my pants pocket and saw that it was Lauren calling. I figured she was calling to apologize so I answered her call on the third ring. "Hello," I said.

"Hey, what's going on?" she asked.

"Nothing much. Just got in the house."

"I know. I just saw you go inside."

"I thought you had practice today."

"It was cancelled."

"So, what's up?"

"Well, I was calling you to see if you were taking me to the Halloween dance?"

"I didn't think you would want to go especially after what happened in the lunch room and all."

"Oh please, that's so two days ago. I am totally not thinking about that girl. She is so beneath me."

"Does that mean that you won't attack her anymore?"

"If she stops texting you then she and I won't have any more problems."

I swear I couldn't believe what I was hearing. Lauren was a hot girl. But she was a bully in the worst way. So, how do I continue to be her boyfriend and have Megan as my friend? Is that possible?

"Hey listen, my mother is calling me to come downstairs and eat dinner. So, give me about a half hour and I'll call you back." I lied.

"Okay."

Immediately after I got off the phone with Lauren I sat on the edge of my bed and thought

about the conversation I had just had with Lauren. Here I was thinking that she was calling to apologize, but she did just the opposite. And at this point I had no desire to go to the school dance.

I knew I had to call Zach and tell him the news but when I was trying to dial out, I noticed that Megan was calling in. I didn't hesitate one bit to answer her call. "Hey Megan what's up?" I asked cheerfully. It was good hearing her voice especially after the call I had just had with Lauren.

"I'm sorry but did I catch you at the wrong time?"

"No. What's up?"

"Well, I was calling you to thank you again for taking up for me at school the other day. None of my friends wouldn't ever stand up for me like that."

"Don't worry about it. Believe me it was nothing."

I'm Just a Normal Kid

"Easy for you to say."

"What do you mean by that?"

"It's nothing." She said and then she paused. "Well, I'm gonna go now so I guess I'll see you in school." She continued.

"Hey Megan wait a minute, would you like to go to the Halloween dance with me?"

"Are you seriously asking me to the dance?"

"Yeah, I'm asking you do you want to go to the dance with me?"

"But what about Lauren?"

"What about her?"

"Dillon, she's gonna scream at me like she did in school the other day if she sees you and I at the dance together."

"Don't worry about Lauren. I'll handle her."

"But what if she gets her friends to bully me?"

"Megan, don't worry about them. No one is going to bother you while you're with me."

"What about your friends? Aren't they gonna tease you for being with me?"

By JC Alexander

"Don't worry about them either. I'll take care of them. So, is that a yes?"

"Dillon, I wanna say yes, but I don't think this is a good idea."

"Why don't you say yes and I'll take care of everything else."

Megan hesitated for a moment and then she said, "Okay, I'll go but you've got to promise me that I won't regret this."

"I promise." I told her. But what I was really doing was putting my foot in my mouth. I couldn't believe that I had just asked her to the Halloween dance. I was so caught up on wanting to make up for the way Lauren treated her that I really didn't think things through. One part of me wanted to uninvite her but then the other part of me couldn't hurt her feelings, so I left things the way they were.

I did however find a remedy for my situation. Before Megan and I got off the phone I instructed her to get her Halloween costume as soon as she

could. I also told her to pick any costume that had a mask. Wearing a mask was an important piece to my plan. I figured that everything would run smoothly if no one knew who Megan was underneath her costume. It would definitely be a win-win situation for the both of us. Lauren or her friends wouldn't bully her and my buddies wouldn't be able to make wise cracks on me.

"Call me as soon as you get your costume, okay?"

"Okay," she said.

I stuck my cell phone back in my pants pocket after I ended my phone call with Megan. I could tell she was excited about going to the dance with me. And I was excited for her too because she was a nice girl and she deserved it. Now all I had to do was figure out what I was going to do about Lauren? How was I going to get out of taking her to the dance without ruining my date with Megan?

By JC Alexander

#Just butter me up
because I might be toast
after all of this is over.

Chapter Twenty-Four
-Zach

"We've got three and a half minutes before the bell rings." I told Dillon. It was critical that I got to class on time today. My parents threatened to ground me and not allow me to go to the dance tomorrow night if I was tardy to any of my classes and I couldn't let that happen. I had a reputation to uphold. And if I didn't show up to that dance tomorrow night no one would have fun.

"Dude, what's up? Have you been sneaking in my sister's room and taking her crazy meds?" Dillon joked.

"Nope. But I have been working on the new and improved Zach."

Dillon cracked a smile. "Sounds like your parents put you in a full-court press."

"How did you know?"

"Come on Zach, I know how your parents get when school events come around. But what they need to realize is that if they stayed consistent you probably wouldn't be so freaking dumb."

"Hey dude, I'm not dumb!"

"Tell that to your teachers." Dillon continued.

"Maybe I should," I said and then I closed my locker.

Immediately after Dillon closed his locker Lauren and one of her friends walked up to us. "Off to class are we?" Lauren spoke up first.

"Yep," Dillon answered.

"Can I talk to you for a minute?" she asked him.

"Yeah, sure." He replied.

When they walked off, Lauren's friend stood there with me, which of course gave me the perfect opportunity to ask her to the dance. Her

name was Erin. And Erin was also a cheerleader. She was pretty but not as pretty as Lauren.

#I guess I gotta be grateful and take what I can get.

"Got your costume for the dance tomorrow night?" I asked her.

"Yep."

"So, who are you going as?"

"A fairy princess."

"That should be cool."

"Yeah, it's a cute costume." She smiled.

"So, who are you going with?"

"I'm not sure. But why do you ask?"

"Well, it would be really cool if you could come along with me."

"Are you asking me out?"

By JC Alexander

"Sounds that way."

"Well, in that case. Sure. I'll go with you."

I smiled at Erin after she gave me a pass to take her to the Halloween dance. I felt like the king of the universe. Now all I had to do was get to all my classes on time so I could make this date a reality.

"Thanks for saying yes. And now I gotta go." I said and ran off to class.

#I love it when a plan comes together. Mission completed!

Chapter Twenty-Five – Dillon

"I know we only have a minute or so before the bell rings, but I need to ask you something." Lauren started up.

"What's up?" I asked her as we walked down the school hallway.

"I wanna apologize to you for the way I've been acting lately."

"Oh really."

"Yes, really. And I want to make it up to you by asking you to go with me to the Halloween dance tomorrow night."

Hearing Lauren say that she wants me to go with her to the school dance tomorrow night was like getting hit in the head with a brick. I was definitely in a jam. And what was so weird about

it was that I knew Lauren was going to drop this bomb on me. So, I came prepared and told her the first thing that came to mind. "I'm not going to the dance." I began to say.

"Why not?"

"Because my parents volunteered me to babysit my little 5-year-old cousin."

"I know that must be a bummer."

"It is because I wanted to go to the dance really bad." I continued to explain. I needed her to see that there was absolutely no way that I was going to be at that dance. So when I did show up wearing my costume and fully masked, she wouldn't be looking for me.

"Wow! This isn't cool. Now who am I going to go with?" she said aloud.

"Why don't you go with your friends from the squad?" I suggested.

"I guess I'm gonna have to."

Before I could add more lies to my conversation with Lauren the school bell rang. "Well,

looks like that's our cue." I said and attempted to walk off but Lauren grabbed my shirt.

"Can I at least get a hug before you go?" she asked.

"Yeah, sure." I said and then I leaned into her and gave her a hug. She returned my gesture with a kiss on the cheek. Immediately after I let Lauren go I noticed Megan standing at the other end of the hallway staring directly at me. I could tell that she wasn't too happy seeing me hug Lauren. But hey, what was I supposed to do? It seemed like I can't win for losing.

#Will I always be a Normal Kid with Girl problems?

When school was over I skated over to Megan's parent's house to see if she got her Halloween costume yet. I knew I could've text her but I

needed to examine her costume in person. I wanted this plan of mine to go off without a hitch. So, I couldn't afford any minor hiccups.

"Did you get your costume yet?" I asked her as soon as she walked outside.

"Yes, my mother took me right after school."

"So, what kind of costume did you get?" I pressed the issue.

"I'm gonna be Catwoman."

"Cool. But does it come with a mask?" I asked her. I needed to know if her identity was going to be fully disguised.

"Wanna see it?" she asked.

"Yeah, sure." I told her.

I stood outside her house while Megan retrieved her costume. And while I waited Lauren calls my cell phone. I quickly answered it. "Hello,"

"Where are you?"

"I'm on my way home. What's up?"

"Nothing. I was calling to see what you were doing."

"I'm on my way home."

"Think I can stop by?"

"Yeah, I'll call you as soon as I get there."

"Okay. Cool. See in a few."

"All right." I replied and rushed to disconnect the phone.

I guess my timing was perfect because as soon as I hung up with Lauren, Megan reappeared with her costume. "Here it is," she said.

I looked at the costume while she held it up. And from where I was standing, it fit all of my requirements. With the exception of my buddy Zach, there was absolutely no way any one would know she was wearing this Halloween costume. "Is it okay?" she asked.

I smiled. "Yes, it's perfect."

"So this means that we're still on for tomorrow's dance?

"Of course. Why do you ask?"

Megan hesitated for a couple of seconds and then she said, "Well because I saw you and Lauren hugging in school earlier so I thought that maybe you were having second thoughts."

"Oh no! Lauren already knows I'm not taking her to the dance."

"Well does she know that you're taking me?"

I couldn't believe that Megan popped this question on me. I didn't know whether to lie or tell her the truth. Telling her the truth would probably do more damage to her self-esteem than anything in the world. So, I took it upon myself to tell her a lie.

#Lying always did the trick for my dad! Up to this very moment, my mother doesn't know that my dad doesn't eat the lunches she packs for him to take to work.

"Yes, she does." I finally said.

Shocked by my answer, Megan said, "Really?"

"Yep,"

"What did you say to her?"

"I told her she was wrong for the way she treated you. And that the only way we could make things right, is that I offered to take you to the dance."

"And what did she say?"

"She was upset in the beginning. But after she sat down and thought about it, she came around and told me I was doing the right thing."

"Are you serious?"

"Yeah, I'm serious." I continued to lie.

"Wow! Really? I mean, Lauren just doesn't strike me as the forgiving type because she's so perfect and walks around school like she can do no wrong."

"If you put it like that, then I can see what you're saying. But trust me, she's okay with it."

After I convinced Megan that Lauren was totally cool with this arrangement, I was able to leave her house. I was literally exhausted afterwards.

Lauren showed up to my house in a matter of two minutes after I got there. If I hadn't known any better I would've thought that she was stalker. "Miss me?" she asked as soon as she stepped into my house.

I'm Just a Normal Kid

"I just saw you in school earlier."

"Will you just say yes? It would make me feel so much better if you did." She said as she grabbed both of my hands in a playful type of way.

"Okay well if it makes you feel better than yes, I did miss you." I replied nonchalantly. This girl was out of her freaking mind. Okay granted, she was hot. But she was insanely over the top too. I mean, how could I miss her when I had just saw her in school a few hours ago? I'm really starting to see that popular girls are much harder to deal with than the nerdy girls. Popular girls are so freaking high maintenance while the nerdy girls are the opposite. Not only that, the popular girls require the spotlight more often and usual.

By JC Alexander

#Maybe I ought to dump Lauren and start going steady with Megan. But will my friends still be cool with me after the fact?

 140

Chapter Twenty-Six – Zach

"So, I hear you're not going to the dance." I said to Dillon the minute I walked up to him at the skate park. He had just gotten off the half pipe so he had his skateboard in his hand and he was drenching with sweat. He and I grabbed a seat on the bench.

"I only told Lauren that so I wouldn't have to take her."

"Dude, you're losing me. So I need you to run it by me one more time."

"What are you mentally retarded or something?" Dillon joked.

"Of course not. I just need you to tell me what's really going on?"

"Well here's the thing, I'm taking someone else to the dance. But I'm keeping it under wraps to keep the drama down."

"Yo' dude, you're so about to create a train wreck."

"No, I'm not. Trust me, this will totally work, especially since I'm wearing a mask."

"You are nuts. You know that?"

"Just chill out. You're overreacting."

"Call me what you want, but I see a disaster waiting to happen."

"Trust me, I've got everything under control."

"So, who are you taking?"

"Promise you won't say anything?"

"Yes, I promise." I lied. I swear, every time he's about to tell me something, he always asks me if I promise and I always give him the same answer. But for a lot of reasons, I always break the code and throw him underneath the bus.

#Thank God he's not a criminal because with my big mouth, a judge would've thrown him in jail and big Bubba would've made him his girl friend a long time ago.

"I promised Megan I was going to take her."

"Are you out of your freaking mind? You can't go to the dance with a geeky girl like her. I mean, what are our other friends gonna say?"

"They aren't gonna know who she is because she's gonna wear a mask just like me."

"You know what? I'm starting to believe that you're the one stealing your sister's meds, be-

cause you've been doing some weird stuff lately."

"Zach, I'm only taking Megan to the dance because I felt bad about the way Lauren treated her the other day."

"Wake up dude! That's what popular girls do. They always pick on the less desirable girls in school. It's been this way since forever."

"Well, it's not right."

"So, what are you, the nerd protector now?"

"No, I'm not. I just want to do what's right."

"Well since you wanna do something right, finish my history report so my parents will see that I'm not jerking off in school."

"Not on your life stud muffin! Call Gabriella. I'm sure she'd love to finish your homework." He shot another Gabriella remark at me.

"Oh go blow yourself! Why don't cha?" I came back on him and then I stood to my feet.

I'm Just a Normal Kid

"Last one on the pipe smells like dog poop!" Dillon shouted as we ran with our skateboards in hand.

By JC Alexander

Chapter Twenty-Seven
- Dillon

Lauren stopped by my house before she left for the school dance. She was fully dressed in her Halloween costume and I was dressed in the clothes I had on in school earlier in the day. Luckily I was already outside goofing off on my skateboard because if she had knocked on my front door, my mother or my sister Julie would've blown the whistle on me and told her they knew nothing about me babysitting my five-year-old cousin. To make matters worse, I could see them letting the cat out the bag that I didn't have a five-year-old cousin to start with. Boy would my life be ruined for sure.

"You look so down and out." She commented.

"I'm cool." I replied.

I'm Just a Normal Kid

"So what time are you going to babysit your little cousin?"

"My dad said that we were going to leave here in about another thirty minutes."

"Boy, I sure wish you could go with me to the school dance."

"I wish I could too. But, look at it this way, since we can't hang out tonight, we'll definitely be able to hang out tomorrow."

"Well, if you put it like that then I guess I'll be okay."

"So, what time are you leaving?" I asked her. I needed to know how much time I was going to have to get ready after she left.

"My mom said we're gonna leave in a few minutes."

"Okay. Cool."

"You know Zach is going to the dance with my friend Erin, right?"

"Yea, he told me."

"Well, I guess I'll be hanging out with them."

"I'm sure you'll have fun. Zach is a major character in his own right."

Lauren smiled. "Unfortunately, I've already seen him in action."

"Lauren, I'm ready honey." Her mother yelled from their driveway.

"Coming." Lauren said.

"Time to go." I said.

Lauren sighed. "I know."

"Call me when you get back."

"Okay." She replied and then she walked off.

I waited for Lauren and her mother to drive away before I went back into the house. I waved them off as they drove by me and as soon as her mother turned the corner I bolted towards my house.

It took me no time to change into my costume. And when I was completely done I looked myself over in the mirror. "You did good Dillon." I whispered.

But before I left the house I called Zach and made sure he was keeping my plans to take Megan out a secret. And after he reassured me that my secret was safe, I hung up with him and called Megan. "Are you ready to leave?" I asked her.

"Yes, I'm ready. But I have one question."

"What's up?"

"You never told me how we were getting to the dance."

"I was gonna ask my dad to drop us off."

"Would you mind if my mother takes us?"

"Oh no, I'm cool with that."

"Okay well we'll be by your house to pick you up in about ten minutes."

"Cool." I said and then we both hung up.

I headed downstairs to the kitchen to get a bottled water and waste a little time before Megan's mom picked me up. My sister Julie and her friend Molly were sitting at the kitchen table surfing the Internet from her iPad. They both

turned their attention towards me the minute I appeared before their eyes. My sister Julie opened the floor by voicing her opinion about my Halloween costume. "I think I could tolerate you more if you wore that costume everyday."

"Yeah, she's right. And I think it fits your personality too." She giggled.

"So, what are you two dressing up as? Hookers!" I snapped back. I had to get those two evil witches where it hurts. They were such nags.

"Mom. Dad. Dillon is calling Molly and I names." Julie yelled.

"Dillon why don't you leave the girls alone?" My mother yelled from the family room.

"They started with me first." I yelled back. But I was so filled up with laughter on the inside. It felt like sweet victory to get back at my sister. Not only had I just scored major points with those drama queens, I even got underneath their skin.

"Get out of here before I kill you!" Julie threatened me as she stood up from the chair.

I grabbed my water bottle and ran for cover. Julie literally ran me out of the kitchen. I didn't stop running until I made it out of the house. "You are dog meat when you come back in here." She roared.

"Oh get a life! And stay off the Internet you porn star!"

Hearing me call her a porn star sent her over the edge. She dashed towards me in a flash. "I am really gonna kill you now." She screamed.

I knew that if she caught me she was going to make me pay. So, I sprinted off in the direction of Megan's house.

By JC Alexander

#Julie had it out for me. She was going to bury me underneath my mother's flowerbed when she got her hands on me.

Chapter Twenty-Eight
- Zach

The school dance was located in the gymnasium. The music was playing and everyone was in costume, including the teachers who volunteered to be the chaperones. Erin was already at the dance with Lauren. As the popular girls of the school, they stood off in their little corner and they owned it. I walked over to where they were standing. "Zach the man is in the house!" I announced myself.

Erin smiled. She was dressed as fairy princess so it wasn't hard picking her out of the bunch. "You look really cute." She complimented me.

"Why thank you." I replied.

"Did you get a chance to talk to Dillon?" Lauren yelled over the music.

"Yeah, I talked to him. Did you?"

"I went over to his house before my mom brought me to the dance. So I was bummed out that he had to babysit his little cousin."

"Me too." I commented. Lauren was visibly upset that Dillon wasn't at the dance with us. But if she knew that Dillon was actually coming and that he was coming to the dance with Megan the geek, she would lose it for sure.

"Come on Erin, let's dance." I said.

"Sure. Let's do it." She agreed.

I escorted her to the middle of the gym floor and did a few moves. I wasn't the best dancer in the world, but I made a dent in the floor. The D.J. was playing "Come & Get it" by Selena Gomez and everyone including myself was going crazy. It was in a good way though.

Thirty minutes into the dance Dillon finally walked in with his geeky date. I knew it was him

because he was the only guy in here dressed in an Iron Man costume. But to make sure I was on my mark I told Erin I'd be back in a moment, then I walked over to where Dillon was standing. "Hey Geek Lover, is that you underneath that mask?" I asked.

"Why of course it is, Mr. Grim Reaper. And to my left is my date Megan." He answered.

"Looks like you two are headed to an old folks convention." I joked.

"Dude, now you know I wouldn't go without inviting you. The old ladies love it when you give them lap dances." Dillon laughed.

"Yeah, yeah, yeah, enough with the jokes. Are you hanging out on this side of the gym?"

"Yep. Don't wanna cause any problems to-night."

"Okay, well I'm going back on the other side with my honey. So, I'll get up with you later."

"Have fun." Dillon insisted.

"I will. Don't you worry." I assured him.

I headed back on the other side of the gym. And when I approached Erin and Lauren they had a lot of questions for me. "Who is that over there with that Iron Man costume?" Erin wanted to know.

"It's my skate buddy Timmy." I lied. Timmy was the first name I could think of. And what was so weird about it was that I didn't know a guy named Timmy. So, I hoped Erin wouldn't probe me with anymore-senseless questions.

"Timmy? I've never heard you or Dillon talk about a guy named Timmy." Lauren yelled over the music.

"That's because we don't hand out that much. He's in the seventh grade." I continued to lie.

#With all the lies I've ever told, it seemed like it was becoming easier every time I opened my mouth. Will it be possible for me to fudge my school records & lie my way into 9th grade next year?

I don't know how I did it but I managed to change the subject from this make believe character named Timmy to the music the DJ was playing. "The last two songs the DJ played were whack." I commented.

"Yeah, maybe you ought to go and tell him to play something hotter like *Lost In Love by Big Time Rush*." Lauren suggested.

"Will do." I told her.

"Can you get me a cup of punch while you're over there?" Erin asked me.

"Yeah, me too." Lauren asked.

"Two cups of punch and a song request are coming right up." I said and walked off.

On my way to the DJ booth I looked across the gym in search of Dillon and saw that he was bopping his head to the beat of the song that was playing. I wanted to go over there and tease him for his efforts in helping the geek with her social issues but I figured now wasn't the time to bust his chops.

Immediately after I grabbed two cups of punch and gave the DJ my song request I headed back to where Lauren and Erin was standing. "Here you go ladies," I said.

Erin smiled. "Thank you." She said.

"Yes, thank you." Lauren added.

I turned back around to face the crowd of kids standing around the dance floor. Every other minute I'd look across the gym to see what Dillon was doing and when I noticed that he had pulled his mask back from his face and leaned over to kiss Megan, I was so shocked that I said, "Oh no Dillon! You're not supposed to kiss her."

"What did you say?" Erin blurted out.

"Yeah, did you just say Dillon's name?" Lauren yelled.

I wanted to answer Erin and Lauren's questions but I was too distracted by what Dillon was doing. And because I wasn't able to pull my eyes away from Dillon and Megan, Lauren and Erin were able to zoom right in on the action.

"Is that Dillon over there kissing another girl?" Erin yelled towards Lauren.

"I don't know but I'm about to find out." Lauren yelled back. Her face turned red as she stormed across the floor. She was definitely on a

mission. So as Erin followed Lauren, I followed Erin.

I tried my very best to flash a signal to Dillon way before Lauren got to him but he wouldn't look up. His attention was so focused on Megan that he couldn't see the hurricane coming his way. And since I was the one to blame for this major screw up, I figured I had to show my loyalty by being there. Who knows maybe I'd be able to clean my mess up.

#It was definitely about to be a WWE Smack-down! Lauren's style!

Chapter Twenty-Nine – Dillon

"Dillon, you lied to me!" Lauren yelled. She stood before me with her arms folded like she wanted to karate chop my head off. I stood there with my mask covering a portion of my forehead and the hair on my head while Megan stood directly beside me with a traumatize expression on her face.

"Dude, I'm sorry. It's my fault." I heard Zach yell.

"Dillon, what is going on?" Lauren yelled once again.

With the music blaring in my ears and the drama unfolding in front of me I wanted to run for cover but I knew Lauren would rip Megan to shreds if I did. So I stood there with all intents

and purposes to do damage control before Megan became road kill right before our eyes.

"I can explain," I yelled so Lauren could hear me over the music.

"I'm waiting," she replied.

To prevent Megan from hearing the lies I was about to tell Lauren I grabbed Lauren's arm and tried to pull her towards the DJ booth. Unfortunately, she wasn't falling for that trick. She pressed her feet firmly against the floor and said, "I'm not going anywhere. You're gonna tell me what's going on right here in front of everyone."

"What do you want me to say?" I yelled. I was trying to buy as much time as I possibly could. I didn't want to sell Megan out in no possible way. She was a good person at heart and I didn't want to destroy it by letting her hear the truth.

"Dillon, I am waiting," Lauren yelled over the music again.

"Yeah Dillon, spill it before Lauren breaks up with you." Erin chimed in.

I was definitely in a tight spot. It was either sink or swim from here!

"This is not what you think." I finally spoke up. But my words were barely audible. I did this with every intention to stall for more time. But once again, it didn't work.

"Dillon, you need to speak louder right now or else it's over between us!" Lauren yelled. Her voice boomed like thunder.

I looked at Zach hoping he'd come to my defense, but he was too preoccupied with Erin. Then I looked at Megan, who by the way was dealing with her own issues, so I knew she couldn't help me either. I was in this jam all by

myself and the way things looked, I knew I had to deal with this on my own.

"Lauren, I don't want you to take this the wrong way but I brought Megan to the dance." I yelled loud enough for her to hear me.

"I see that! So, why did you lie and tell me that you had to babysit your little cousin?" she yelled back.

"Because I had already asked Megan to come to the dance." I yelled.

"You mean to tell me you asked that geek to the dance?" Lauren yelled. She was grinding her teeth so I knew she was steaming on the inside. To tell a popular girl that you asked a nerdy girl to the dance before her was rare. That almost never happens.

"I only asked her to come to the dance to make up for the way you treated her the other day."

"Oh so you're doing charity work now?" Lauren continued to yell.

"Yes, if you want to call it that." I said without realizing what I was saying. And then I went on to say, "So, it's your fault. If you would've left her alone you and I wouldn't be having this yelling match."

"You're kidding me right?"

"No, I'm super serious." I assured her. And then I turned my attention towards Megan, who by this time was about to have a freaking meltdown.

She literally stood next to me with a massive amount of tears falling from her eyes. I tried to comfort her but she pushed my hands back. "Don't touch me." She yelled and then she stormed off.

"Hey Megan wait, don't leave." I yelled and turned to run behind her. I knew I had hurt her feelings deeply so I had every intention to console her.

By JC Alexander

#Megan didn't ask for this madness. But somehow or another she got pulled in it anyway. Talk about peer pressure!

Before I could move a good two steps Lauren grabbed the back of my costume. "You are not going anywhere." She yelled.

I stumbled a bit trying to catch my balance. And when I was standing firmly on my feet, Lauren stepped towards me and started yelling in my right ear. "If you run behind her, it's over between us."

I thought about what Lauren had just yelled in my ear. She gave me an ultimatum. I had to choose her or Megan. What was I supposed to do?

 166

Chapter Thirty-Zach

Megan ran out of the gymnasium and didn't look back. Dillon stood there clueless. For the first time my best buddy acted like he didn't know how to handle a girl. And the fact that Lauren stood over top of him like a bully didn't help the situation. I stood there with my date Erin and wondered what was Dillon going to do next.

By JC Alexander

#In all honesty, it was more painful to watch Dillon make a complete fool out of himself than for me to get a flu shot!

"Come on Erin, let's get out of here." I said.
"Wait Zach, I can't leave Lauren like this," Erin spoke up.

"Oh she's a big girl! She'll be fine." I assured Erin.

#Dillon was my buddy and all but I spent a lot of money on this Halloween get-up. So, I had to get my monies worth.

I grabbed Erin's hand and escorted her to the dance floor. I wasn't about to waste any more time harping on some one else's date. My dad always told me to make the best out of every situation. And that's what I planned to do.

"Party over here!" I yelled as I walked onto the dance floor.

While Erin and I were jamming on the dance floor, she pointed out how Lauren and Dillon were still in the same spot we left them.

"Do you think they're gonna break up?" Erin yelled in my ear.

By JC Alexander

"I don't know." I replied.

"What do you mean you don't know? Look at Lauren. She's beautiful and popular! That nerdy girl's looks don't come close to Lauren."

#Erin was right, Megan's looks don't compare to Lauren's looks. Lauren was like a goddess! Megan was a nerd! So, why did Dillon bring Megan to the dance instead of Lauren? I'm thinking that maybe his mother must've dropped him on his head at birth & now he's suffering from brain damage.

The Halloween dance was going to be over in an hour so Dillon had to make up his mind if he wanted to be with either Lauren or Megan.

He was definitely a Normal Kid with Girl Problems.

The End

By JC Alexander

COMING SOON

I'm a Normal Kid with MORE

Girl Problems

Part 2

Find out what happened to Megan
after the dance...

Who did he choose Megan or Lauren?

 172

CRUSH LETTER

DEAR _____,

MY NAME IS _____.
YOU MAY NOT HAVE NOTICED BUT I'M IN
YOUR _____ CLASS. I'M A VERY
COOL PERSON SO I WOULD LIKE TO
KNOW IF YOU'LL HANG OUT WITH ME AT
THE SKATE PARK OR THE MALL?

CIRCLE YES OR NO

Having problems with your boy friend?

Is he always at the skate park with his friends? Or is there a boy in school you want to go out with?

Don't worry Megan and Lauren are here to help. Post your question and they will answer it as soon as they can.

Having problems with your girl friend?

Or is there a hot girl in your school that you have a major crush on?

No problem, Dillon is here to help. Post your question and he will answer it as soon as he can.

CONTACT THE AUTHOR/
FAN MAIL:

K.S. PUBLICATIONS
C/O J.C. ALEXANDER
P.O. BOX 68878
VIRGINIA BEACH, VA 23471

OR LOG ONTO:
WWW.IMJUSTANORMALKID.COM